# HANS HOFMANN

FRUIT BOWL, 1950
Mr. and Mrs. Roy R. Neuberger, New York

# HANS HOFMANN

BY FREDERICK S. WIGHT

UNIVERSITY OF CALIFORNIA PRESS

Berkeley and Los Angeles : 1957

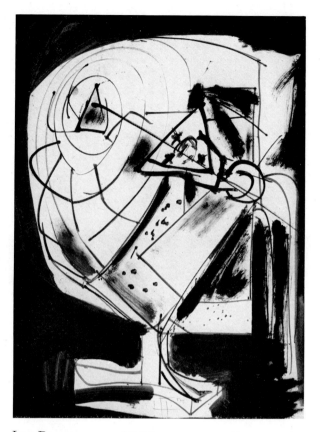

INK DRAWING, *ca.* 1945
Collection of the Artist

UNIVERSITY OF CALIFORNIA PRESS
Berkeley and Los Angeles, California

CAMBRIDGE UNIVERSITY PRESS
London, England

© 1957, by The Regents of the University of California

Printed in the United States of America
by the University of California Printing Department

Library of Congress Catalog Card Number: 57-7593

Published for the Art Galleries, University of California, Los Angeles

Designed by Adrian Wilson

THE OCCASION RESPONSIBLE FOR THE PUBLICATION of this book is the Hans Hofmann Retrospective Exhibition, organized by the Whitney Museum of American Art, New York, in association with the Art Galleries of the University of California, Los Angeles, and shown in 1957 and 1958 at the following participating institutions: Whitney Museum of American Art, New York; Des Moines Art Center; San Francisco Museum of Art; Art Galleries, University of California, Los Angeles; Seattle Art Museum; Walker Art Center, Minneapolis; Munson-Williams-Proctor Institute, Utica; Baltimore Museum of Art.

Thanks are due to Bartlett H. Hayes, Jr., for permission to quote from his biographical study of Hans Hofmann in *Search for the Real*, published by the Addison Gallery of American Art, 1948; and to Clement Greenberg for the excerpts from his critical essay printed in the catalogue of the Hans Hofmann Retrospective at Bennington College, 1955. Appreciation is expressed to *Arts and Architecture* magazine for permission to reprint "The Color Problem in Pure Painting—Its Creative Origins," by Hans Hofmann.

We are grateful to Time, Inc., for making available the color plates: RED TRICKLE and SCOTCH AND BURGUNDY; the Albright Art Gallery: EXUBERANCE; the University of Illinois: BURST INTO LIFE; the William H. Lane Foundation: EMBRACE; the Whitney Museum of American Art: MAGENTA AND BLUE; and to William Kaufman for the reproductions of the mosaic at 711 Third Avenue.

Credit is extended to Arnold Newman for the photograph of Hans Hofmann, and to Percy Rainsford for the photographs of ELEGY, GERMANIA, and LIBRATION.

FLOWERING BRANCH, 1953
Mr. and Mrs. Gifford Phillips, Santa Monica, California

# CONTENTS

# FOREWORD

Hans Hofmann's art is a controlled explosion. Whether he deals directly with nature or with the reasoned structure of cubism or with the freer forms of present-day abstraction, the exuberance of his brush shatters the normal limits of style and creates its own dynamic order. The vitality of the man and of his art is indivisible. Even his titles—*Ecstasy, Burst into Life, Ascop*—are words that explode or escape the bounds of dictionary English.

His work is inimitable, as many of his students have discovered, yet Hofmann has been a great teacher to those who catch fire from his enthusiasm but reserve the strength to find their own way. As both teacher and artist, he has been a perilous and a liberating power in our twentieth-century art— perilous because his illusion of unleashed force has sometimes been mistaken for a gospel of emotional license, liberating because the true strength of his art lies in an iron self-discipline, which alone justifies the extravagance of his experiments.

That nothing is impossible so long as the creator controls his means is an ancient lesson, but one that Hofmann proves more dramatically than most living artists. He has opened new avenues to the future, and they are not even, necessarily, those that he himself has so brilliantly explored.

JOHN I. H. BAUR

*Photograph by Arnold Newman*

X–1955

Mr. Peter A. Rübel, New York

# HANS HOFMANN

## BY FREDERICK S. WIGHT

Hans Hofmann, at seventy-six, is a spectacle of health and exuberance, a man of a compelling physical amplitude. Rubens might have brushed him in; visibly he is a product of the baroque spirit. He is glowingly affectionate, fluent, amiably authoritative, and philosophically explanatory in a language of his own, an English that has not ceased to be German. He nudges his phrases along with the constant persuasive "nicher" (a Bavarian condensation of "nicht wahr"), as though he were always in search of an answer. To approach Hofmann is to enter a metaphysical world of his own creation—what he calls his cosmology—a way of seeing the universe. Soon you begin to feel that philosophy or faith as an external fact, and to see Hofmann as a Copernicus who has placed the sun where it belongs. He has found a solar role for color.

Hofmann is one of the few colorists Germany has produced. His paintings are resplendent outbursts; the light and blaze are explosive. The canvases look new in the world, a fresh part of creation, and this is much the fact. Hofmann's art, as it has significantly developed, is recent—a matter to be accounted for. A paradox: here color seems to live for its own sake, if ever color did, but in reality it is color for the sake of form.

**13**

Hofmann's painting has a rational history. It is a French-disciplined painting which, as it has come to reveal itself, is entirely un-French. Yet it is certainly a latter-day development, a culmination, of Fauve painting, and a reasoned development out of cubist painting as well—Fauve primarily, put to a new and larger use. The time lag is no greater than the change in aspect, as of Romanesque art going over into Gothic, or high Renaissance into baroque.

This outpouring coincides with a recent turn in American art. How much abstract expressionism owes to Hofmann, or Hofmann owes to the support of a general movement, is not easy to determine. He did not suddenly become a cubist among cubists. It seems plausible that Hofmann has gained as much from the slow absorption of the past as from the stimulus of the present, and has grown out of a tradition that has gradually become his own. His painting is based on a long-labored philosophy, the work of a mind temperamentally akin to the scientist's. Hofmann lives in a world of tensions and balances, of implied further dimensions, and his rationality is as determined as the stroke it controls is frenetic. There are painters who feel the need of accounting for what they have done. Hofmann, on the contrary, appears as a man who first needed the accounting, who had first to convince himself. Subsequently— perhaps years subsequently—he had to paint his concepts.

Styles and movements are measured by decades in this century, and an artist may be expected to outlive his way of seeing. It now seems normal to watch an artist painfully explore, achieve, retreat, and then change direction. Cubists did not always remain cubists, and abstract expressionists will (or do) painfully change direction too. In the midst of all these explorations, these shifts of balance and recent recollections of lost images, Hofmann seems deeply committed to his vision, and it is difficult to see him treating his own painting as one of many possible ways. He is almost the prisoner of the faith that has liberated him. His painting is not only what he does, but what he is forced to believe. This fact somehow attaches a further validity to his work, if only that he has paid a higher price. In a time of uneasy change, such an amount of dogma—of hard-won self-faith—is impressive. As a teacher, Hofmann has been justifying his faith for many years and, to quote Bartlett Hayes in his biographical study, Hofmann's school is his pulpit.

Hofmann begins with what he blandly calls his cosmology: his sense of the universe as a field of force, or a series of such fields, loose-knit. It is a universe of separate galaxies, presaged emotionally in the sky of van Gogh's STARRY NIGHT. The plane of the canvas cuts through this massive concept like the

**14**

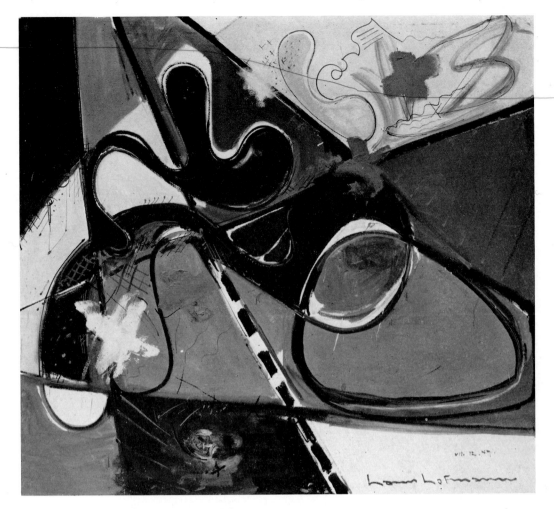

SUBMERGED, 1947
Collection of the Artist

plane of the ecliptic. The plane itself organizes the depth above and below, its two dimensions serving to capture a third otherwise beyond grasp. And these depths are not conceived as figures and numerals (for Hofmann is really an artist and not a scientist), but as forces and pressures transmuted into light and color. In Hofmann's metaphysics, tensions of a cosmic order can translate into the tensions of feeling. But this is a vital and not a passive process. We are close to Schopenhauer's World as Will and Idea.

Does this make Hofmann's painting better? Belief wins battles. In the course of time, Hofmann has moved from anguished uncertainty to boundless assurance.

**15**

Idolatress, No. 1, 1944
Collection of the Artist

Hofmann is an intensely active man: teacher and painter the year round. He conducts his long-established school, on Eighth Street in Greenwich Village, has his studio around the corner, and lives within walking distance on West Fourteenth Street. His studio is workroom and storeroom, on fire with paint. His apartment is illuminated with splendid canvases—those he understandably wishes to keep close—although none is safe in its present state while it remains under his eye. Each may still undergo transformation.

For five months in the year Hofmann and his wife leave New York for their home in Provincetown on the tip of Cape Cod. His students follow him, a new summer crop of students springs up, and his didactic life begins again. In Provincetown Hofmann has more time to paint, and it is here that he has produced most of his impressive recent work. The white shadowless light of the shore is better than the light in the city. Here too, Hofmann has territory to call his own, with all frustrations painted out.

It is the American custom to segregate the arts. Certain favored towns are saturated with artists in summer, and become colonies in the bacteriological sense of "colony" or "culture." Provincetown is one of the oldest colonies of this kind, chosen for its picturesqueness as a fishing port in the days when the severe architecture of New England and the gaunt structure of the seafaring New Englander were the literal artist's stock in trade. The cluttered and congested town consists of two long streets connected by the narrowest lanes, and the houses on the shore side of Commercial Street trail down onto wharves, brick underpinning making way for piling. Large white churches give an impressive lift to the snug architectural scale, as do the windowless cold storage plants—the morgues of the fishing industry. The place has a considerable Portuguese population, which adds a Latin flavor and perhaps gives some faint relevance to an outsize Florentine campanile idiotically erected to the Pilgrims, who landed here before they found solider footing over by Plymouth.

Provincetown once had its fishing fleet, and I recall watching the gray, two-masted schooners standing solemnly out to sea for the last time and heading for the Banks. This fleet eventually joined forces with the one from Gloucester and moved to the rival port. The rivalry with Gloucester continues, but it is of art colonies now. The business of Provincetown has long been art, a product manufactured under the eye of the curious and merchandised on the spot.

In these circumstances, at once encouraging and humiliating to ability, a number of artists have won respect and reputation. Many have schools, for Provincetown abounds in students. Hofmann's school is, however, not a local development; it dates from the Munich of 1915, a pioneer movement in the teaching of modern art. As such, in New York and Provincetown, it provides Hofmann with a following. He is a simple-hearted man who sees things his own way, longs to share his beliefs, and expects and wins loyalty. His students are counted in the thousands now, and they are fiercely believing disciples.

Complete with school, Hofmann lives in the extreme west end of Provincetown, at home in a captain's house built long ago, foursquare and ample, for a man of self-respect. The clean, white house sits well back from Commercial Street and looks across the harbor. Inside a white gate the hollyhocks grow tall on each side of the brick walk, and tie the blue of the sky to the blue of the water. This is Hofmann's headquarters as truly as it was the original owner's, of whom there is nothing reminiscent to be seen. Hofmann has moved in and provided for his own needs without compunction, and the effect is good, as of two strong personalities getting along together.

Indoors, there is a steep central stair, with a square room on either side and a passage to the long room across the back. The interior is as white as the shingles, except for the floors, which are variously a clear, stinging blue, apple green, mustard yellow, and a wonderful tomato red. After this exercise, the eyes are ready for the paintings. The living room is given a lift by the large golden IDOLATRESS, the larger RED AND BLUE INTERIOR, and WICKER CHAIR, No. 2. In the one-time parlor to the west hang two portraits, of the very young Miz Hofmann and of the artist, which date from 1901 and 1902. It should be said at once that there are other paintings beside Hofmann's. The front room to the east is hung with a collection of Vivins, blue-gray primitives that record every stone of Paris and serve as a foil to the owner's bold constructions. The living room contains a Miro, a small Braque, and a smaller late landscape by Renoir.

Hofmann, the physical man, organizes this space around him by his presence. He is entirely willing to be intruded upon and overrun; his Bavarian affability and his availability are inexhaustible. It is not enough that he offers his ideas and his inquiring blue-eyed glance—the whole man appears to be offering his whole self. Hofmann wears clothes of a most domestic casualness: a loose, colored shirt, open and short-sleeved, seems to be peeling away like so much sunburn; his elephantine trousers are equally flimsy and ample; and his sandaled feet are as much in evidence as his hands for the solid capable working parts that they are. The man is a complete, full-bodied entity, all of a piece, whether he is tirelessly pattering about in search of something that will

**18**

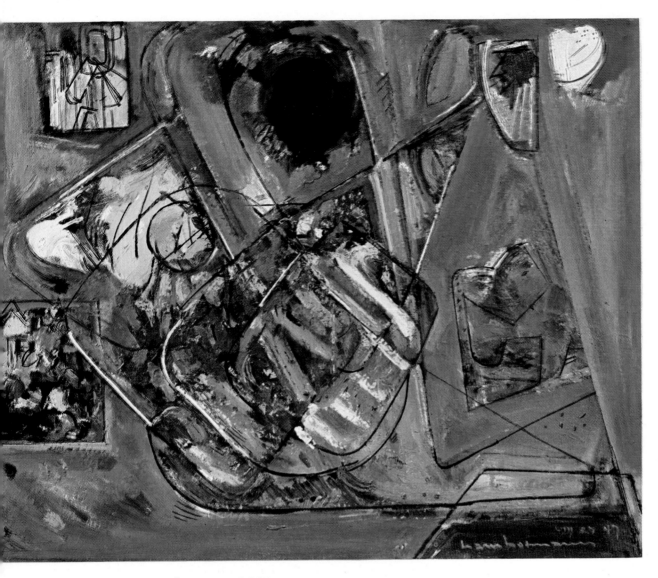

INTERIOR, 1947
Dr. Fred Olsen, Guilford, Connecticut

help him explain, or sitting rocking his shape into the upholstery of a chair.
He wears a hearing aid, which seems to protect the subjectivity of his thoughts
and to put a little strain on his attention and a little time lag before his smile.
In winter, when he is flannelly and woolly, he conveys the impression that his
clothes are a pelt.

The scene around him is crisp and orderly. This is the bailiwick of Mrs.
Hofmann, who provides marvelous food when it is time for food, accurate
records when records are required, and, perhaps, ambition if ambition is

**19**

MRS. HANS HOFMANN, 1901
Collection of the Artist

needed. "I was very, how do you say, *populaire*, when I was young," she confesses. So she still is, and will always be.

Hofmann has his double purpose in existence: to paint and to explain. It is curious, therefore, that the explanation took up the first half of his life and that his important painting came last. Only after he came to America did his talent come clear. The early evidence has been largely lost, to be sure: he left his earliest work in Paris in 1914 and never saw it again; his later paintings left behind in Germany have not apparently survived the last war. The Hofmann emancipated from the image (although he will argue the image in and out of his canvas—"I have never given up the *object*") is a relatively new man and, it is tempting to say, a young one. The Hofmann before our eyes in the present tense is determined on a still better bargain with life; he cheerfully points to Titian, who painted until he was ninety-nine.

There is enough of the best of Hofmann's work in this house, to say nothing of the studio, to chart his course, and to watch the *object* sink below the horizon until you are at sea in color: in this fluid and tumultuous world you are lost for lack of a landfall, and you must navigate, appeal to the universals of geometry and the stars—in short, turn to an ordered cosmos.

To return for a moment to the early portraits—Miz Hofmann was painted compactly before the young artist knew of impressionism, yet his own boldly painted head of the next year is almost postimpressionist, the dots and stabs free as Signac's. Then there is a long time gap, to be filled by drawings of 1925 or 1926 from the south of France: fluent, rushed, in the manner of a man who knew the cubist procedure but, like Matisse, chose not to make use of it—content instead to remember the old testament of Cézanne. The paintings begin again in 1935; a loose, violent naturalism, the forms separate and distinct, whether of hills or buildings, and tending to be written in with separate colors, form by form.

TABLE WITH DRAPERIES (1936), in the living room, is a clear and legible still life, with color beginning to grow arbitrary according to the painter's needs. The whole thing is lacerated with fishhook forms, a sharp handwriting serving equally as a description of the object and as Hofmann's signature. This painting stems from the artist's experience of Paris early in the century. It is Fauve, for all the cubism it contains; it has the French order and the German excitement.

On the opposite wall, TABLE and WICKER CHAIR, No. 2 (1942) show the development in the next six years. Gaining freedom, Hofmann grew impatient with an even balance between concept and event. His choice was weighted heavily in favor of arrangement in color, and the image was gradually overwhelmed.

SELF-PORTRAIT, 1902
Collection of the Artist

BIRTH OF TAURUS, 1945
Mr. and Mrs. Fred H. Olsen, Guilford, Connecticut

There is a parallel with Kandinsky's departure from naturalism some twenty-five years earlier, and a certain resemblance too in the final result, when freedom has been won. But the resemblance to Kandinsky is never close enough to embarrass. Kandinsky and Miro have a wide channel between them through which many painters besides Hofmann can pass. The basic postcubist Hofmann is a master of rugged geometry, the paint sculptured into great glowing blocks—in such a painting as SCOTCH AND BURGUNDY, for example. And there is a symbolist Hofmann of ferocious images, of gargoyles or harpies—such is the IDOLATRESS (1944). The Hofmann of 1947 who painted the rare, transitional canvas, PALIMPSEST, is master of whimsical images that are snared with a light line.

"If I take it from nature, I paint it very quickly," says Hofmann. "Those from the imagination take longer." In the present decade, the contrast, formally, is between structures that create the illusion of powerful machinery colored so as to make its working plain and paintings that are all impulse and tumult. Technically, there is the contrast between the slightest of stains, the brush trailing lightly over canvas, or paint caked on until the whole surface is painted desert, dried and throbbing in the sun.

At all times Hofmann is concerned with the third dimension, creating a sense of depth, pressure, and mass, as though reminding us that the surface of the earth is not only a hovering plane but a crust over a boiling vat. "I found my own way to present the object in pictorial giving, not perspective giving, nicher?" Hofmann takes on an air of intense seriousness, and explains once more, as he has for the better part of his life:

"That was my whole influence on my students, years before . . . The object should not take the importance. There are bigger things to be seen in nature than the object. To become higher expressive, something must be suppressed. . . . But I have never given up the *object*. When you analyze nature in regard to a picture, then the object is absorbed through light, or shadow, or color, to create more interesting shapes than the object offers. We must stay *above* and not *below* nature.

"A picture must be made, dictated, through the inherent laws of the surface. I invented what I call 'push and pull,' force and counter-force. I have been very modest about it, but they are really great discoveries. The highest three-dimensionality is two-dimensionality, which no layman can ever understand. Depth is nothing less than suggested volume. I have students who come to me painting in two-dimensional rhythms, an empty affair.

**23**

"Everything you produce must be integrated. That is the first condition that you can speak about in a work of art. That makes pictorial vitality, nicher? Not only do things shift on the surface, but *depth* must be suggested.

[Question: "How will your painting develop from here?"] Towards qualities that are still stronger, still more expressive, still more alive than they are today. ["Through simplification?"] A very important thing. I say to my students, you must give with the least the most, not with the most, the least. A thousand leaves are still not a tree, a thousand flowers not a bouquet. Greater you should go, simpler you should go. But simplicity should mean pureness, not poorness. People try to go simple but go empty. The essence of my school: I insist all the time on depth. Suggestion of depth. That is the reason that I discipline my students from nature. In the beginning with the figure—the model.

"This is what I stress in my teaching: No perspective but plastic depth."

Hofmann demands of the surface of his paintings that ominous, kinetic sense of depth that underlies an ocean of cloud seen from a plane in flight. This depth he creates out of the tensions between colors and shapes. In

AGGRESSIVE, 1944
Collection of the Artist

Hofmann's phraseology, a certain combination of colors and shapes in a given area is called a *complex*, a galaxy of forces in play, which contrasts, and sets up tensions, with another related complex in another area of the painting. Granted that these explanations are figures of speech (although, like most philosophers, Hofmann probably takes his concepts for an actual account of circumstances), there is a hint here of a way of seeing his own past. Certain significant events add up to a complex that conditions the next complex brushed in at another time in a new country. Descartes' theory of vortexes would be a better scheme for Hofmann's life than a rigid three-dimensional frame. We had best let Hofmann teach us, and try to create an impression of depth for him, without getting lost in perspective.

A few early facts and impressions indicate a childhood extrovert to a degree in contacts with people, isolated in puzzlement over what Hans Hofmann was to do with his life. He was born in Weissenburg, in the Bavarian countryside, on March 21, 1880. Shortly afterward, Hans' father received a government appointment that took him to Munich. He was "an officer in the Government"— a bureaucrat by employment and apparently by temperament. There were five children, three boys and two girls, and Hans was the second son. It was a close-knit group, but: "My father was a peculiar man, not interested in the family. He did not maintain a strong contact with the children; he was quite severe. It was the mother who was the bond."

Hans' mother was the daughter of Frederik Manger, who was a "brewer and a wine-producer," with hop fields and vineyards along the River Main in northern Bavaria. In Bartlett Hayes' account of Hofmann's early days, much is made of the boy's relation to this grandfather, of whom Hofmann speaks with affection and respect. There were baskings and broodings when the young philosopher meditated on the nature of reality, quite in the German tradition, while he watched the disturbance of the canal reflections—one reality disrupting another—as the barges went slowly by. Farm life here was almost medieval, too prosperous and comfortable for sudden change. The field hands ate at long tables at harvest time, and the young grandson appeared as a privileged and important figure in this bland and orderly feudalism. Hans was musical, but perhaps no more than his whole environment was musical. He played the violin, the piano, and the organ. His was not a solitary temperament.

The boy, with his diffuse and expansive nature, seems to have been appreciated by everyone but his father. He was packed off to school, where his

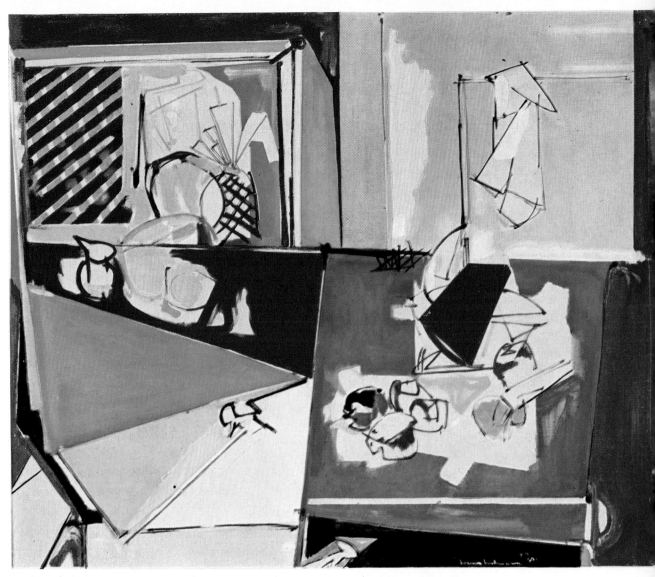

MAGENTA AND BLUE, 1950
Whitney Museum of American Art, New York

aptitude for mathematics and science mended matters, but it was plain that
the narrow realism of his father's career was not Hans' reality. Gradually he
outgrew the constrictions of his life at home, and at sixteen he broke away from
his family and never returned to it. In retrospect Hofmann sees his escape as
no more than the natural emergence of a free spirit. "In those days, the boys
broke away and the girls stayed in the family, nicher?" How did he live and
manage at that age? Soon his father found him a "beautiful job in an architectural and engineering office in the government," where he worked until he
was eighteen. His father smuggled money to him indirectly through a friend.
"In those days, money was still *gold*."

**26**

Hofmann's reference to gold opens the story of his invention of an electromagnetic comptometer. His mother had to sign the application for a patent, since the self-educated engineer was under age and he would not allow his father to help him. His father, impressed and pleased, congratulated his son through an intermediary, who "poured a stream of gold upon my desk—a thousand marks." The sum might well have been spent on a laboratory; it extended possibilities and added to Hans' indecision. But he had begun to draw and paint, and finally he invested in tuition. He registered in an art school.

"Also," says Hofmann, "people recognized my talent and supported me." The young Hofmann, like the young Kokoschka, seems to have been able to secure from the world at large that generous support that parents usually provide. He was handsomely staked by a patron for many years. Surely this easy capacity to make society a parent tells much, and should be remembered in connection with the warm parental relationship of Hofmann to his students, after he himself became a patriarchial figure. He seems to have been able to carry his family feeling out into the world around him, so that temperamentally he has never been out of family life. In Munich he met Miz Hofmann, when he was twenty-one and she was sixteen and a half. She had, according to Hofmann, "a little money and no parents." It is certain that she had infinite charm.

Two other facts: when Hofmann was twenty-two, his father died; also, a brother was a suicide, "because he forgot to break away."

For a time the young Hofmann was student, amateur scientist, and inventor. Hofmann, impressed by a shipwreck much in the news in 1898, "experimented with high-frequency radiation" and produced a signaling device to warn vessels of unseen dangers. He also worked on an electric bulb, sensitized by "exposure to extremely high potentials" so that it glowed faintly without any source of electricity. This was intended for coal miners. Next, he devised a portable freezing unit to preserve food on military maneuvers. None of these inventions paid off, but the young Hofmann was imbued with a scientific view of nature and saw the world as a rational interplay of forces. His imagination was not stopped by the screen of visual appearances.

Many years were to go by before there could be a synthesis between such a view of nature and the organized tensions on canvas that Hofmann was to create. As an art student, he learned what he was taught, and he was taught very traditional things. The names of his teachers are dim now: Michailow, Aspe, the Hungarian painter Ferenczi, and Grimwald, who had quite an influence, as Hofmann concedes. More important to him was his last teacher, Willie Schwarz, who had been in Paris and who came back full of a new discovery—impressionism. "One must observe nature by means of the light reflected from objects, rather than be concerned with the tangible existence of the objects themselves." Here was an opening for the scientific spirit. Colors were vibrations of a certain frequency; a color pattern, which was all that the eye experienced, was therefore an exercise in the combination of numbers. So Hofmann became an impressionist.

Hofmann too wanted to go to Paris, and Willie Schwarz provided not only the incentive but indirectly found the means. He introduced his student to the nephew of Phillip Freudenberg, the Berlin collector, a nephew who, as Hofmann says, "was related to other people who had supported me." Freudenberg, owner of a Berlin department store, paid Hofmann's fare to Paris and continued to support him for ten years until the outbreak of the first World War. Such an act of confidence is to the credit of both men, and presupposes a determination and conviction on the part of the young artist—a belief in himself that was to make life difficult for him, to keep him struggling, to prevent him from painting like the many other artists he met in Paris.

Hofmann made his way directly from the railway station to Montparnasse. He entered a café and by signs obtained bread and coffee; he read the name of the café upon leaving, so that he could return. It was the Café du Dôme. Here gathered the well-known names of an epoch—but they were not well known then. The year was 1904. These men were living in poverty, determination, and hope, swept along by their confidence in their experiments, in their ideas, and by their addiction to the new. The Fauve movement was just under way, and the cubist discoveries were still to be plotted. These artists could be spoken to. They too were young, and many were soon Hofmann's friends—Matisse, Braque, Delaunay, Picasso, and Juan Gris—to be known with varying degrees of intimacy. The outrageous Pascin was known well and at once. Hofmann had come ahead to Paris by himself. "Pascin and I never went home at night at all. Coming back in the morning, I was often disgusted to the bones, and I thought it would be better to jump in the Seine. Six months later, I went to Knocke, in Belgium, to meet Miz. We were together from then on."

One of the earliest and strongest influences upon Hofmann was Matisse—the kinship survives in Hofmann's freedom as a colorist. He worked alongside

**28**

YOUNG WOMAN, 1927
Collection of the Artist

Matisse in the evening classes at Colorossi's, and he was greatly impressed by Matisse's JOIE DE VIVRE. Hofmann once painted in the Hotel Bisson, on the quai des Grands Augustins, on the same balcony where Matisse painted his famous early views of the Seine. It was a severe winter—there was no heat in the hotel, and Miz Hofmann had to stay in bed to keep warm while Hofmann painted on the balcony. Marquet also painted in this studio, and Delaunay, living nearby in the rue des Grands Augustins, was a close friend. Of all the painters Hofmann knew in Paris, he was closest to Delaunay in friendship and in ideas. Then too, Mme Delaunay was German, and Delaunay played an important role as liaison between the French and German painters. Klee and Franz Marc knew him, and he had his influence in Munich before the war.

Hofmann watched the coming of color in Delaunay's work. The transition from the grays of Delaunay's SAINT SEVERIN to the color of his Eiffel Tower painting paralleled Hofmann's own development as a colorist. Hofmann had come to Paris at the right time to assimilate the color and freedom of the Fauves. No sooner was this revolt into color established, however, than Braque and Picasso were evolving the cubist discipline. Hofmann embraced this new interest and became absorbed in cubism. An acquaintance with both Braque and Picasso dates from those years.

RED TRICKLE, 1939
Miss Irene Manning
New York

What did Hofmann actually paint?—still lifes, of course, landscapes in the Luxembourg Garden, and figure pieces. It was a time of "deep, deep struggle," of discovery and growth, rather than of production. To the young Hofmann, a mere theory of art was insufficient. With his scientific bent and his German instinct for a total philosophy, he had to account for everything at once. He was organizing images, but they were still images; the art that was to prove right for him was far in the future.

No painted record of those years exists. The canvases in Paris were abandoned, and lost with the coming of war. A considerable number were sent to Phillip Freudenberg in Berlin in return for his generosity, but Hofmann's patron later fell on evil days, and these paintings have also disappeared. When Matisse was given a show in Berlin by the dealer Cassirer, he saw the Hofmanns belonging to Freudenberg, and Matisse's enthusiasm had the

**30**

convenient effect of encouraging Hofmann's patron to continue his support. Doubtless there was friendship in Matisse's response, but Hofmann's paintings were able to stand without assistance. Hofmann showed in the New Secession in Berlin in 1909, and the next year, when he was just thirty, Cassirer gave him a one-man show.

In Paris, the Hofmanns lived in Montparnasse in the rue Campagne Première; later they were in the rue de Sèvres. Summers they went back to Germany to Herrsching and to Ammersee. Early in 1914 Hofmann's sister was seriously ill, and he went to Munich to be with her. He stayed, of course, for the summer, and was caught in Germany by the outbreak of the first World War.

Hofmann spent the war years in Munich. An old lesion of the lung disqualified him for service in the army, and he had to work out a life for himself in spite of the war. Paris had provided him with ideas, and he needed to bring order to them and to enlarge them—in short to make them his own. In 1915 he opened a school and became a teacher, and a teacher he was to remain.

There is a problem here—a problem of definition of what a man really is. It seems clear that the effort of his mature years was given primarily to teaching, and equally clear that he is now, first and foremost, a painter. To be sure, the activities have fused, and Hofmann's ultimate style is so imbued with a point of view or a concept of art that it can almost be seen as a concrete philosophy, a plastic thinking. But it is irresistible to speculate on the length of time it took Hofmann to become his own follower and to fulfill his own prophecy.

There are points of resemblance to Gropius, who was to set up the Bauhaus four years after Hofmann opened his school. However they differ, both men presented the same division of interest between performance as artist and dedication as teacher. Both live in a "total" philosophy of their own, a world larger than their particular art, in which, however, this chosen art is allowed to play a preponderant part. It is tempting to see a didactic philosophizing as something essentially Teutonic, as though there were a need for some vast rational matrix to restrain or to balance the intensity of impulse. Perhaps there is something in the German temperament even more Freudian than philosophic: the revolt against excessive paternalism and authority leads the revolutionary to set up his own government and become lawgiver in turn.

The artist may quail, and be left with his anxieties. But he can choose his own battleground, if he has the ability to create a world of his own to master and defend. Charlemagne is the Teutonic archetype: once a man is strong enough to crown himself, authority, no longer the enemy, comes marvelously to his aid, and all else follows.

Hofmann, then, lifted himself out of his "deep, deep, struggle" through his years of teaching, which served to clarify his belief, and—more than that— thrust upon him a parental role until at length he grew into the patriarchal figure that he needed to be. His freedom is of a peculiar order: that of a liberated intuition firmly based on the justifications of rationalized authority. It is not surprising that his feeling for universals, for concepts, in a field where others offer only temperament and idiosyncrasy, has won for Hofmann a large following to the present day. From the beginning, his school was an immense success.

The school was in the suburb of Schwabing. It was wartime, but in 1915 it was a successful war. Hofmann had some hundred students, mostly women. He explained the principles of cubism, and he inculcated a visual order. His whole school was in a sense an abstraction, an abstraction from the times. Hofmann has always been obsessed by the feeling of the religionist: that people are living outside the significance of their epoch and that it is within his power to bring this significance to them. He had no time to paint—there was to be little painting for nearly ten years, not until 1924. But he drew continuously; it was part of his teaching. Bartlett Hayes conveys admirably the dedication behind Hofmann's teaching in those war years:

"One afternoon in the fall of 1918, he began to wonder if he shouldn't abandon the crusade. His energies had been exhausted while promoting the welfare of others. His own work had suffered. His teaching was now a chore instead of a stimulus. He argued with himself a long time, standing by the window as darkness came on. He watched the brightening stars, now one, then another, then several more. Each new star changed the pattern ever so slightly, for, as it appeared all the rest moved over, as if by common consent, to readjust themselves in his vision and make room for the new. This organizing and reorganizing of twinkling points of light seemed much like painting. Just as in vision, each planet was in actual tension with every other in the system—in relative tension that caused it to swing in an unseen orbit, obeying unseen laws, even into translucent infinity. If one looked long enough, these relationships and hidden forces appeared even more real than the array of the stars themselves. The difficulty with material things on earth was that they were generally too close and too familiar to be readily sensed according to their

DELIGHT, 1947
The Museum of Modern Art, New York
Gift of Mr. and Mrs. Theodore S. Gary

GREEN BOTTLE, 1921
William H. Lane Foundation, Leominster, Massachusetts

true related significance. Of course, painters could, if properly trained, make allowances for false impressions of vision. Yes; it would be right to continue the school, to continue it at all costs.

"He lowered his eyes to the city. Suddenly, flashes of fire showed beyond the housetops, as if flowers had fallen from the firmament. What strange stars were these? The fireworks continued to celebrate for several hours. The anguished years of war had ended."

Hofmann's school began to be known abroad, and there was an influx of foreign students. The school became international. Art itself took on a new value: here was one field where there was no defeat. Yet the times were still full of trouble: revolution flared, and there was a more serious kind of fireworks. A large city goes about its business all the same. Revolution was exhilarating, and the liberal spirit was full of hope. The days of organized injustice were far ahead.

In summer Hofmann took his school into the mountains on the Austrian frontier. These movements added to the identity of the school—and its identity with its founder. No one had traveled during the war, and soon Hofmann was carrying his students further afield. In the summer of 1924 the school was at Ragusa in the new country of Yugoslavia. Then for the next three summers—1925 to 1927—Hofmann took his school to Capri. For the summers of 1928 and 1929 he moved his students to a soberer locale: the still unexploited Saint-Tropez. The south of France offered a landscape structuralized—classicized—in recent memory by Cézanne. Art is international, and Hofmann was glad to be back in France. For that matter, he had made frequent trips to Paris since the war, and was again in touch with many of his old friends.

Hofmann had once more begun to paint. A canvas, GREEN BOTTLE (1921), survives in the collection of the William H. Lane Foundation. The painting shows a familiarity with cubism; it is most consciously built. And from the summers in Saint-Tropez there are naturalistic drawings that have a cellular organization, the mind guiding a rapid hand. These were more than note takings: they described an artist who could combine the structural with a lyric freedom.

A new kind of trouble, meanwhile, had been fomented in Munich. Life was to grow difficult for venturers in ideas. Hofmann, with his international following, was vulnerable. Fortunately, he had an opportunity to come to America. Professor Worth Ryder of the University of California, Berkeley, who had been a Hofmann student, was responsible for an invitation to teach at the summer school at the university.

The interest in Hofmann at Berkeley was also due to Professor Glenn Wessels, who studied with Hofmann at Saint-Tropez. Edgar Rupprecht (who later came to the United States) was then translating Hofmann for the benefit of his students, and Wessels undertook to teach Hofmann English. Wessels went to Munich to be his assistant during the winter of 1929. Their sessions were from six to eight in the morning "each correcting the other," and it is conceivable that Hofmann taught more than he learned. It was Wessels who "brought Hofmann over," and fended for him in his lectures; together they wrote a book which has never been published.

As a result, Hofmann taught in Berkeley in the summer of 1930, and when his term was over he was invited back for the following year. His influence in Berkeley was strong and immediate, and has survived. Erle Loran has written about Hofmann, and many Berkeley students have gone on to study with him.

Hofmann went home, and came back in the spring of 1931, teaching first at the Chouinard Art Institute in Los Angeles before his second summer in

SAINT-TROPEZ, 1927–1928
Collection of the Artist

Berkeley. In August the California Palace of the Legion of Honor gave Hofmann a one-man exhibition. There were no paintings—it was an exhibition of drawings, almost a third done in California, the others dating from the summers at Saint-Tropez. This was the first one-man show since the exhibition in 1910 at Cassirer's gallery in Berlin. Some release was at work in Hofmann, some need to redefine himself against a background totally new.

In the autumn of 1931 he came to New York to teach at the Art Student's League, and the following summer he was instructor at the Thurn School in Gloucester. It was the familiar pattern—except that the schools were not his own. He opened a school in New York that autumn on Madison Avenue, but his teaching was interrupted in the spring by a trip to Bermuda "because of visa trouble." After a few months' rest he returned on a permanent visa, which served until he obtained his citizenship.

He was back at the Thurn School in the summer of 1933, and in the autumn of that year he put his New York school on a more permanent basis and relocated it at Lexington Avenue and Fifty-seventh Street—there were to be further changes of address, first to 52 West Ninth Street, then to Eighth Street in Greenwich Village. In 1934 he took his students to Provincetown and set up a summer school of his own. He was again teaching the year round at a

**36**

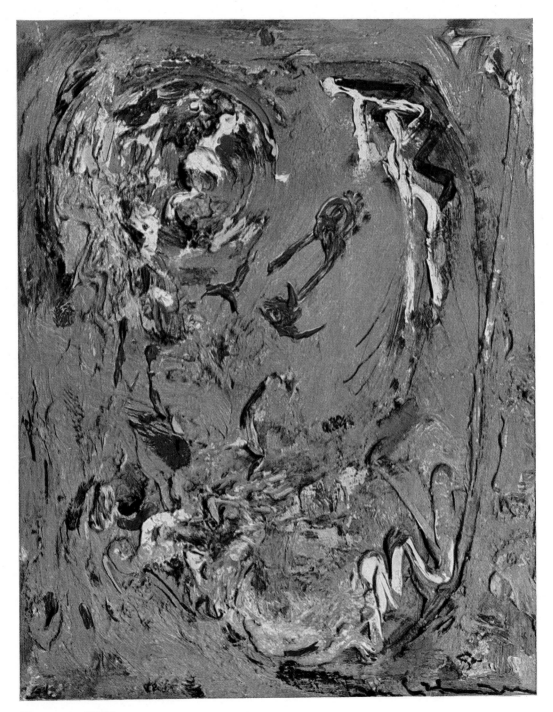

Bouquet, 1951
Mr. and Mrs. William Sachs, New York

school of his founding—a function that had taken five years to bring to America from Europe.

The Isaac Delgado Museum in New Orleans gave Hofmann a one-man show in 1941. It was ten years since his last exhibition in San Francisco, yet the paintings that were eventually to place Hofmann in the forefront of the newest movement in American art were all in the future. Hofmann had completed their necessary forerunners. His canvases of the 'thirties were all landscapes or still lifes named for recognizable subject matter. TRURO RIVER (1936) and PROVINCETOWN HARBOR (1939) were not too different from the pen drawings of Saint-Tropez. The forms were packaged with colored line; distinct colored areas were only beginning to assert themselves. The breakthrough, however, was at hand. RED TRICKLE (1939), or such an after-the-fact title as THE POET (1940), indicates the extent to which subject matter was being transformed. IDOLATRESS (1944) presents an image recognizable yet grotesque, a figure of contemporary mythology, a phoenix on fire in its yellow

PROVINCETOWN WHARVES, *ca.* 1940
Collection of the Artist

DEVELOPING COMPOSITION, *ca.* 1940
Collection of the Artist

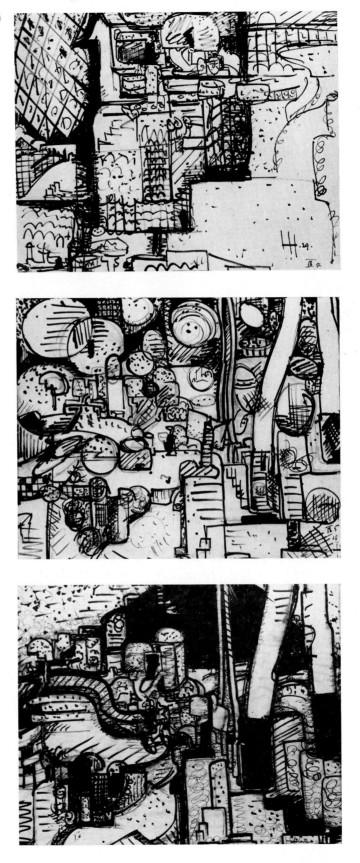

EMBRACE, 1947
Lane Foundation
Leominster, Mass.

blaze. EFFERVESCENCE, the Addison Gallery of American Art's BLACK
DEMON, and SUMMER GLORY were exceptional paintings of this date.

Release and recognition coincided. In March of that same year, 1944,
Peggy Guggenheim had given the artist a one-man show at her Art of This
Century Gallery in New York. The announcement carried a statement in
Hofmann's most exuberant vein: "To me creation is a metamorphosis. The
highest in art is the irrational. . . . incited by reality, imagination bursts into
passion the potential inner life of a chosen medium. The final image resulting
from it expresses the All of oneself." Little here of Hofmann's inherent laws,
of which he now feels himself master.

There was another important exhibition in the autumn of the same year at
the Arts Club of Chicago. Then the gallery showings began in New York: at
the 67 Gallery that same autumn (1944) and in the following spring; at the
Betty Parsons Gallery in the springs of 1946 and 1947; and in the autumn
of the latter year came the first of the annual showings at the Kootz Gallery.
With these exhibitions Hofmann was inevitably identified, perhaps in spite of
himself, with America's painters of the subjective experience.

**40**

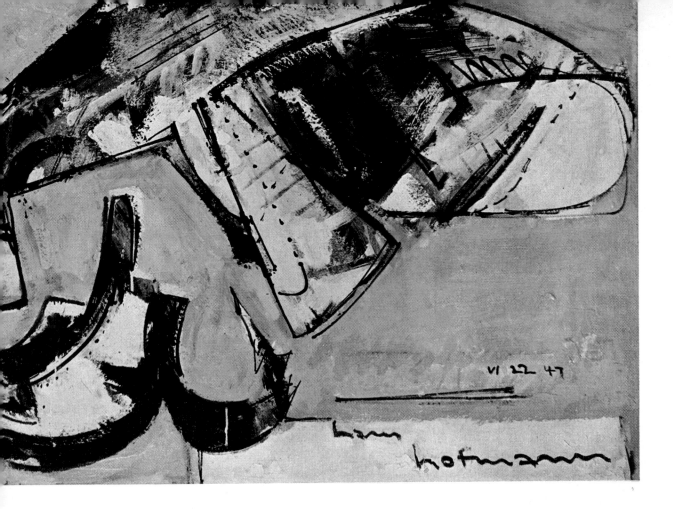

BIRTH OF TAURUS (1945), now in the Fred H. Olsens' collection, owes its organic power to the excitement of creation: this is the present tense; the artist offers the sensation of painting rather than the result of painting. DELIGHT (1947), in the collection of the Museum of Modern Art, is more orderly, more under the control of Hofmann's postcubist discipline. Here the painter establishes forms that are half living, half man-made, a sort of machinery in man's image, a projection of man himself through his ideas. The forms move upward from both sides of the canvas, and the result is sculpture-because-of-color. Hofmann is not a colorist in the sense that color is an end in itself; he is a powerful user of color as a means.

Painted in the same year with DELIGHT are: COURTSHIP, a black-and-white oil, which can stand for a small group in which Hofmann eschews color altogether, as if to prove that he can create formal tensions without color as his fourth dimension; and EMBRACE, a strong abstract gesture, in the collection of the William H. Lane Foundation—a collection in which Hofmann canvases begin with GREEN BOTTLE (1921), continue with EMBRACE, BLACK LIGHT (1947), and COMPOSITION, No. 7 (1953).

GERMANIA (large version), 1951
Baltimore Museum of Art

The Kootz Gallery showing had hardly concluded in December, 1947, before a major retrospective opened, on the following January 2, at the Addison Gallery of American Art, Phillips Academy, Andover, Massachusetts. Bartlett Hayes, the director, had assembled "fifty years of paintings and drawings from 1898 to the present day, arranged to show the growth of a personal, aesthetic philosophy." The exhibition was presented as a special study, aimed at an audience of every age; it was conceived as instruction, and Hofmann's teaching was implicit in the presentation. The timing was right: the Hofmann we now know had at last emerged. Even paintings like the recent PALIMPSEST appeared as intermediate steps, and APPARITION, AWAKENING, and SEATED WOMAN established the powerful new language.

As a result of the exhibition, Bartlett Hayes produced a volume, *Search for the Real*, in which Hofmann wrote down his doctrine. The artist's text is followed by "excerpts" from his teaching; and Hayes' own monograph, with the explanatory legends to the illustrations, achieves an extraordinary identification with Hofmann's point of view, and carefully fills in the intermediate steps vaulted by the painter's intuition. Not ten years old, this excellent work reminds us how much persuasion of the public was still needed at so recent a date.

**42**

In the following January (1949) Hofmann returned to Paris, after many years, with an exhibition at the Galerie Maeght. The exhibition was a large one, with forty-four items. Seated Woman, Summer Glory, Libration, and Submerged are familiar by now. In the Maeght publication, *Derrière le Miroir*, Charles Etienne, under the title *Hofmann ou la Lumière Américaine*, concluded that Hofmann may claim as his own that "vitalité scandaleuse avec quoi il represente, comme rarement on l'avait fait jusqu'ici, cette prodigieuse, irrespectueuse (malgré les apparences) et toujours neuve Amérique . . ." The flamboyant "Appreciation," by Tennessee Williams conceals a calm statement: "He is a painter of physical laws with a spiritual intuition." This seems to state the case.

The 1950 showing at the Kootz Gallery, with nineteen paintings, included the brilliant Fruit Bowl of the Roy and Marie Neuberger Collection, a powerful target in red-white-green. Magenta and Blue (1950), now in the Whitney Museum's collection, conveys the Hofmann intensity through cacophony: the painting, basically a still life, divides into four areas, organized as "complexes" out of red, yellow, and green that are, so to speak, then taken for granted and set over against the intrusive "magenta," whose hostility must be absorbed. In 1950 and 1951 the gallery catalogues make mention of Hofmann at seventy. If there is any hint of conclusion here, it has been dropped, as Hofmann has continued to gain in boldness, assurance, and power, his annual autumnal exhibitions blazing forth like the fall turning of the maples and oaks.

Elegy, 1950
Walker Art Center, Minneapolis

SCOTCH AND BURGUNDY, 1951
Samuel M. Kootz Gallery, New York

1950 seemed primarily a year of geometry, and so was 1951, with its outstanding SCOTCH AND BURGUNDY. 1951 also produced manic paintings: BURST INTO LIFE, GERMANIA, and PERPETUITA. The canvases of the 1950's are in general more lyric and less structural, unless you seek the structure in the sculpture-in-paint, as the artist almost literally weights the surface and seems to be composing in depth by means of the differing specific gravities of the colors on his palette. COMPOSITION, No. 10 (1953), belonging to the Abbott Laboratories, has massive pigment that makes us apprehend depth, just as there is a rhythm in the surface of the ocean (as opposed to the rhythm in shoal water), which tells us we are off soundings.

In ORCHESTRAL DOMINANCE IN YELLOW (1954), in the Mr. and Mrs. David M. Solinger Collection, and in EXUBERANCE (1955), in the collection of the Albright Art Gallery, the painter is "giving up one thing for another thing," and his goal is clearly intensity. Ideally, the enjoyment of a Hofmann painting should be in the observation of its creation, watching the "complexes" develop and seeing the complexities proliferate, only to be overwhelmed by

**44**

ORCHESTRAL DOMINANCE IN YELLOW, 1954
Mr. and Mrs. David M. Solinger, New York

some element of the artist's selection: for, in spite of appearances, the artist's drive is to overcome differences, to indicate an enormous sum total, and then to simplify and condense. Perhaps Orchestral Dominance in Yellow most completely describes, even in title, the painter's accomplishment

The Orange Vase (1955), belonging to Mr. and Mrs. Charles S. B. Ward, with its heavy paint, revolves around a still recognizable fragment of reality. If Hofmann begins with an arranged still life—as he often does—this reliance on nature is more than a convention. He is insisting that his "subjectivity" is not a private world, but a personal understanding of the larger world, a transcript of outer forces.

The Baltimore Museum of Art gave Hofmann a one-man exhibition in 1954, including the large Germania, which the museum acquired. Hofmann says in the catalogue: "Art . . . glorification of the human spirit . . . cultural documentation of the time in which it is produced." His statement has a highly autobiographic conclusion: "The deeper sense of all art is obviously to hold the human spirit in a state of rejuvenescence."

Bennington College held a symposium on art and music in the spring of 1955, and fittingly dramatized it with a Hofmann retrospective: the twenty-two paintings covered the years 1938 to 1954. Summer Glory (1947) again catches the eye, as does Blue Enchantment (1951), of the Mr. and Mrs. Fred Olsen Collection. Libration (1947) is a powerful abstract pattern, which asks the imagination to recognize figures and the gesture between them. The painting belongs to Mr. and Mrs. Samuel M. Kootz.

The Bennington catalogue carried an essay, by Clement Greenberg, of a lucidity not always present in writings on Hofmann, which sometimes compete in language with Hofmann's exuberant use of paint. Greenberg rightly stressed the Fauve in Hofmann: "The result was not an eclectic, composite art, but was an organic fusion evincing qualities that were new and not foreseeable either in Matisse or cubism." Greenberg sees also a parallel to Paul Klee: "Klee was the first, consciously, to broach painting as matter of addressing oneself to the responsive rather than inert or passive object constituted by a plane surface. He conceived of painting more as the prodding, pushing, marking and scoring of a surface, than as the inscribing, tracing, or covering of it. Hofmann found his own way to the same approach. In practice even more than in precept, he reveals the picture surface as something alive and needing only to be touched to show its life—as something that quivers to the touch, and throbs and breathes in answer to paint." There is a note of defense of the

**46**

"open, pulsating paint surfaces. . . . As his thickly painted pictures dry out, and their colors come closer together in key, they become smoother, firmer in their unity, more traditional in their resonance, and their force becomes more compatible with elegance. It is perhaps too soon for the standard good taste of our time to see this." Hofmann is in recently overrun territory that is not altogether pacified.

If it has taken so long for Hofmann's art to command its present frontiers, it is only reasonable to expect a certain restiveness from the noncombatants, the neutrals. It is also true that such a strenuous and vital performance presents temperamental difficulties for the lovers of art who are not always lovers of life. Hofmann's active bulk makes something of a fool of those impelled to discover—for he is not to be found under a leaf. Finally, the didactic Hofmann is ever ready with his statements, and he has a way of taking the word from those who have only words to offer.

LIBRATION, 1947
Mr. and Mrs. Samuel M. Kootz, New York

ORANGE VASE, 1955
Collection of
Charles S. B. Ward
Pittsburgh

There is something disarming about the exuberance and extravagance of the names that Hofmann chooses or invents for his canvases—until you realize that the titles are somehow right. Hofmann's art is entirely joyous—although the images may be fierce—and there is far more here than a Bavarian guilelessness: there is hard-won confidence that comprehension spells power. This belief parallels one of the few optimisms of our time, that knowledge exorcises guilt; and Hofmann shows you a chromatic world as it might be felt and understood with a good heart. You reflect that the disturbances and anxieties that so often accompany ability are illnesses after all, even if they are so widespread that they set a pattern. There seems to be no remnant of malaise in Hofmann, and this is all the more remarkable in a man who has transplanted himself into circumstances very different from those he first knew. But in Hofmann there is still the boy of sixteen who could leave his own family so easily because he was at ease in the larger family. It is the nature of good health to live in the present with an eye to the future, to be earthy, and at home anywhere on earth.

**48**

The activity of painting comes first, before the exhibitions and the words; a studio is simply the workshop where it happens. At Provincetown, inland from the shore, and at some distance from Hofmann's home, there is a coal-and-lumber yard flanked by a long two-story shed, the second story reached by an outside stair and catwalk that leads past the studio doors. One of these doors is Hofmann's. The room is square, not large, the light coming from above the door and from the back, although two large easels block the rear light. The right-hand wall is stacked with canvases, either new and waiting or freshly painted and leaned against each other with the greatest care, for the thick corded paint will be drying all summer. On the opposite wall—white plaster broken through to the lath—are small reproductions of the Christ of Avignon and of a Giotto over against a T-square and saw that make a pattern on the plaster, for this is a practical place.

Move back from the easels: before you have enough distance, you are against a table whose glass top is a palette. There are paints in an enamel tray, brushes of every size grow out of jars like bamboo, and after the largest come the still larger housepainters' brushes. Hofmann, as he is now explaining, often works from preliminary studies in gouache, which are dashed off in series as he encourages the growth of an idea. Then comes—or may come—a linear design in thin color on the canvas. Or color blooms in stains, establishing planes and areas. Then perhaps a profusion of prismatic little chips and triangles appears, and the painting grows scintillating, furiously complex. Later, all this is likely to be simplified and heightened. The canvas will resolve itself into balanced areas, "my complexes," which create a sort of equilibrium of pressure. These complexes tend to employ the same color relationships, and so compose; or they come to be dominated by one major color-form event, a central solar fact that holds all the satellite areas in place.

Hofmann explains, gesticulating, his hand going over the canvas as though repeating the original attack. He uses musical terminology: "Thirds, fourths, fifths, how do you say? We make an octave, what is the word?—blue here, you look for another blue—nicher—yellow starts here, one here, the eyes are permanently guided in a rhythm, each color has its own rhythm. In the end this leads to the re-creation of forms."

In the end, Hofmann leads us to his extraordinary freedom out of a sense of mastery, to a confidence that there is nothing incompatible between control and release—one makes possible the other. He leads us to one of the positive painting events of our time; and to a denial that life is tragic.

**49**

FLORAL COMPOSITION, 1954
Mr. and Mrs. Norton Simon, Los Angeles

## THE COLOR PROBLEM IN PURE PAINTING—
## ITS CREATIVE ORIGIN

The genuine value of a painting is greatly determined through its basic concept.

In painting we differentiate between "pure painting" and "tonal painting." Pure painting is the antithesis of tonal painting.

We deal with tonal painting where color is degraded to a mere black and white function through its use as a means for tonal gradation from the highest light down into the deepest tonal shades. Tonal gradation can be produced by any kind of color mixture.

In pure painting color serves simultaneously a plastic and psychological purpose. We deal, in the achievement of this purpose, with a formal problem and with a color problem in parallel occurrence, the synchronization of which constitutes the pictorial synthesis of the work. Color has in itself a sovereign function on the basis of its intrinsic qualities. Color in itself is Light. In nature, light creates the color; in the picture, color creates light. Every color shade emanates a very characteristic light—no substitute is possible.

The luminous quality of a work depends not only upon the light-emanating quality of every color but predominantly upon the relation of these particular

**51**

qualities. Relation is the product of hypersensitive creative mind. Relation produces a new quality of a higher order through a created actuality, either in the form of tension, when we deal with the compositional demand of integrated form, or in the form of intervals, when we deal with color relations. We must always distinguish between *form* in a physical sense (nature) and in an esthetical sense (the form of the work itself—as created by the mind).

Pictorial life is not imitated life; it is, on the contrary, a created reality based on the inherent life within every medium of expression. We have only to awaken it. Color metabolism preconditions the continuity of color development towards a plastic and psychic realization. Continuity of color development is achieved through successful, successive development of the color scales. These are comparable to the tone scales in music. They can be played in Major or in Minor. Each color scale follows again a rhythm entirely its own. The rhythmic development of the red scale differs from that of the blue scale or the yellow scale, etc. The development of the color scales spreads over the whole picture surface, and its orientation, in relation to the picture surface, is of utmost importance.

The formal development of the work and the color development are performed simultaneously. The color development leads thereby from one color scale to the other. Since every color can be shaded with any other color, an unlimited variation of shading within every color scale is possible. Although a red can be, in itself, bluish, greenish, yellowish, brownish, etc., its actual color emanation in the pictorial totality will be the conditioned result of its relationship to all the other colors.

Any color shade within one color shade can become, at any moment, the bridge to any other color scale. This leads to an interwoven communion of the color scales over the entire picture surface.

Whereas in tonal painting neighborhood relations are achieved through dark and light transitions, in pure painting the rhythmic interweaving of the color scales brings the color into an "open" neighborhood relationship in which colors are compositionally in accordance with a color development upon which their formal grouping ultimately depends. The colors meet now in neighborly relation in the sense of tensional difference—that is to say, in the sense of simultaneous contrast. The finest difference in color shades can achieve powerful contrasts. Although tonal development may lead to an overall pictorial harmony, it sacrifices simultaneous contrast, which is the predominant quality of pure painting.

A painting has an immediate impact, but is conceived sequentially. The process of development is made invisible in the synthesis of the completed work.

Looking at a picture is a spontaneous act that reveals at once the quality or non-quality of the work.

But what is quality? Quality is the essence resulting from convincingly established felt-relationships. It can only be produced through an act of empathy, that is, the power to feel into the nature of things.

In color, the establishment of relationships is based upon the possibility of the multi-shading of colors. Their rapport, unlimited to local areas, spreads over and dominates the whole picture surface.

Color is, of course, not a creative means in itself. We must force it to become a creative means. We do this in sensing the inner life by which related colors respond to each other through the created actuality of intervals.

An interval is the physical precondition from which arise the hyper-physical overtones governing the sensitive relations of two physical carriers upon the canvas. It is analogous to a thought-emotion fragment in the creative process through which an idea is made communicative.

Intervals are tensional variations, the degree of which characterizes a given relation. In a relation, two colors engage each other in a simultaneously accelerated intensification or diminution. None is the winner and none the loser. Both are united to carry a meaning through their interaction. The divergency in both makes the tensional difference of the interval.

An interval can function in the sense of a second, a third, a fourth, etc. Like sound in music. This characteristic makes color a plastic means of first order, since painting is a continued process of color-development, its ultimate aim being the creation of maximum volume expansion into the depth, combined (but in counter action to it) with utmost contraction. From the counterplay of both these forces emerges the ultimate monumentality and the plastic synthesis of the work.

But expansion-contraction is not exclusively a color problem. It goes hand in hand with the play of Push and Pull in the formal development of the work. Push and Pull control not only the variations of depth relations in a two-dimensional sense, but especially the variations of intensities in these relations. The most pronounced depth suggestion is then enriched, in the painterly process, by greater voluminosity, which generally requires a deeper shading of color with a consequent diminution of luminosity. Lesser formal depth

**53**

suggestion demands diminution of volume and intensification of luminosity. This statement should not be considered an inflexible rule. Nevertheless not only two-dimensionality established itself in every instance of form and color development, but also balance of luminosity and volume.

Painting has many problems, but the foremost is the synchronized development of both form and color. Both developments are esthetically identical in their relation to the picture plane, the nature of which I have fully explained in a previous essay. (See New Ventures No. 1—or the catalog of my previous show [1954] at the Kootz Gallery).

To resume:

1) Color, in its over-all function upon the picture surface, becomes in the development of the picture, subject to an ever changing multi-interpretation.

2) Color must sustain its own development: it is, per se, a color development problem.

3) It is the color development that determines the form. Color has, besides its own development, a formal function. It places itself (as a consequence of its own development) in plastic relation to the picture plane. This formal back and forth in the composition produces a painterly equivalent which adapts itself in the reversed direction (in the sense of compensation). Color attains in this way an active part in that magic phenomena of push and pull which creates the pulsating quality of pictorial life.

4) The color development explained in the foregoing process determines also the neighborhood function in which two color shades meet each other in a neighborly relation, not in the sense of tonal transition but in the sense of simultaneous contrast. Their meeting is the consequence of the color and the form development of the work. Both go hand in hand, but form and color (and the latter in a multiple sense) operate each in its own sovereign rhythm.

The characteristic of every great work of art is simplicity. In its final state, the color development over the whole picture surface leads to the creation of color—or light—complexes. The composition is thereby dominated by a few such complexes only.

In a complex, a few, a greater number or a multitude of colors (or color shades) meet to produce this effect. In spite of a multiplicity of shaded differences, their synthesis presents itself as one color complex contrasted with another and all the other color complexes within the pictorial totality. All complexes have an inter-response through the intervalled relation of their inner buildup. When this is not the case a number of pictorial fragments will

**54**

EXUBERANCE, 1955
Albright Art Gallery, Buffalo

appear, with no unity towards pictorial totality. The picture exhibits holes, with the disturbing effect of showing two or a greater number of isolated pictures on the same canvas.

A color complex presents volume in a multitude of color vibrations. In pure painting we deal always with created color in the sense that jewels create color. A ruby is red—an emerald is green, a sapphire is blue, a topaz is yellow, etc., and they retain their color identity in every change of normal light-condition. But when we analyze the red or the yellow or the blue in these precious stones then we find that we deal not with a simple red, yellow, green or blue, but with a multitude of prismatic-differentiated colors which, in their gathered intensity, create in us the idea of the ruby red, the sapphire blue, the topaz yellow, the emerald green, etc. In pure painting the interplay of the color leads to the creation of the intended effect of a blue, a red or a yellow and the total harmony between them emanates the aspired creative intention. This concept differs from another concept by which greatly simplified decorative areas are desired. This concerns the art of elimination. In the decorative domain of the color it must be understood that any color mixture becomes a pure color when the mixture is thoroughly flat-mixed, so that it carries only one light meaning. Great areas can be handled in this way when such simplified areas respond in the sense of intervals also.

To conclude:

Pictorial life is a created reality. Without it, pictorial communication— the appeal to the senses and the mind—is non-existent. Color (in nature as well as in the picture) is an agent to give the highest esthetic enjoyment. The emotion-releasing faculty of the color related to the formal aspect of the work becomes a means to awaken in us feelings to which the medium of expression responds analogically when we attempt to realize our experiences creatively. Upon it will depend the formal and psychic appeal of the created image which is finally achieved through an absolute synchronization, in which a multitude of seemingly incompatible developments have been firmly interwoven: molded in the synthesis of the work.

Endowed with such cognition, all creative possibilities are left open to the imagination, inventiveness, and sensibility of the artist, and to the selective capability of his mind.

Being inexhaustible, life and nature are a constant stimulus for a creative mind.

56

Mosaics, 1956 (Northeast corner)
711 Third Avenue, New York

# HANS HOFMANN

## AS A MURALIST

Le Corbusier, in setting the outer limits of a work of architecture, states that the composition stops at the horizon—a conclusion to which he came on seeing the Parthenon on the Acropolis. Such an expansive concept inevitably makes of an architect a city planner. There is something of such an expansiveness in Hofmann's paintings; they ask that their way be cleared, call for white walls and brilliant floors, as in his home in Provincetown, or at least for sufficient space for their orbits. An architect's space is not a matter of cubic feet merely, but of what is done with that space, of how it is transposed into the space of the imagination. In the home of the designer Charles Eames, two Hofmanns are hung as horizontal planes from the two-story ceiling of the living room. As you sit in the room and glance up, the circular patterns on the square canvases—one white on red, the other white on blue—become separate vortexes in space. Unlike mobiles, which move with the stirring air, these paintings seem to set up a circular current in the air around them.

On a much larger scale, Hofmann's new mosaics in the lobby of the Kaufman Building in New York, designed by the architect William Lescaze, aid immeasurably in the transformation of the architectural environment into that imagined space over which our painter has such special control. Here is recognition of the fact that this transformation of space—the essence of archi-

**58**

tecture—is not completed until all possible visual resources are brought into play. Indeed it is not complete until the building is inhabited and so becomes an experience in time revolving around the people within it.

That Hofmann has worked successfully in mosaic is not surprising, since he often achieves a lapidary effect with his heavy, coruscant pigment; and there is a rightness about the increase in scale, as though this were at last life-size work for Hofmann, the natural growth and development of an art able to thrive in an architectural climate.

The adaptation of abstract expressionist painting to architecture seems so natural that we must remind ourselves that it is no more natural than anything else in art. The connection was seen and realized in large degree by Samuel Kootz, who, as a dealer, established liaison between teams of major architects and artists. This goes back to an exhibition in 1950 in which Hofmann took part. The architects with whom Hofmann collaborated were José Luis Sert and Paul Lester Wiener, and their project was the civic center for the newly planned city of Chimbote on the coast of Peru. The bell tower for the church was designed as a free-standing slab fifty by twenty-four feet, to be entirely surfaced with a Hofmann mural; the mural was planned to compose with a mosaic of natural stone on the floor of the plaza. Projects such as these, the work of talented and successful men, were not destined to remain mere exercises, and it was not long before a number of artists were being employed to work with architects on plans that came into being.

F. S. W.

Mosaic of about 1,200 square feet, commissioned for the lobby of 711 Third Avenue, New York. Owners of the building: Mr. B. H. Swig, Fairmont Hotel, San Francisco; Mr. J. D. Weiler, 711 Third Avenue, New York; Mr. William Kaufman, 711 Third Avenue, New York. William Lescaze, F. A. I. A., Architect.

The builders and their architect determined upon a "work of heroic size, the central portion of a very busy new building, making available to the public an unusual piece of art by an equally unusual modern artist."

Mosaics, 1956 (Southwest corner)
711 Third Avenue, New York

# HANS HOFMANN

## CHRONOLOGY

| | |
|---|---|
| 1880 | March 21: born Weissenberg, Bavaria, Germany. |
| 1886 | Family moved to Munich. Attended public school and, later, gymnasium. |
| 1898 | Began to study painting in various art schools in Munich. |
| 1904 | Work seen by Phillip Freudenberg, department store owner and art collector in Berlin. Freudenberg's patronage enabled him to go to Paris, where he stayed for ten years. |
| 1914 | At outbreak of World War I, home on vacation in Munich. Kept out of army by aftereffects of lung ailment. Freudenberg's assistance terminated by war. |
| 1915 | Opened art school in Munich. |
| 1924–1929 | School taken on summer trips: Ragusa, 1924; Capri, 1925–1927; Saint-Tropez, 1928–1929. |
| 1930 | Taught summer session, University of California, Berkeley. Returned to Germany. |
| 1931 | Spring: taught Chouinard Art Institute, Los Angeles. Summer: taught again, summer session, University of California, Berkeley. |
| 1932–1933 | Taught Art Students League, New York. |
| 1932–1933 | Summers: taught Thurn School, Gloucester, Massachusetts. |
| 1933 | Opened own school in New York. |
| 1934 | Opened summer school, Provincetown, Massachusetts. |
| 1941 | Became an American citizen. |
| 1944 | First exhibition in New York arranged by Peggy Guggenheim, Art of This Century Gallery, marked turn to abstract expressionism. (*See* Exhibitions.) |

**61**

## AWARDS

1950  University of Illinois, Champaign-Urbana. Purchase Prize.
1952  Contemporary Art Society, Chicago. Purchase Prize.
1952  Pennsylvania Academy of Fine Arts, Philadelphia. T. Henry Schiedt Prize.

## EXHIBITIONS

(One-man shows, unless otherwise noted)

Paul Cassirer, Berlin, Germany: 1910
California Palace of the Legion of Honor, San Francisco: 1931
Delgado Museum, New Orleans: 1940
Art of This Century Gallery, New York: 1944
Arts Club of Chicago (retrospective) : 1944
67 Gallery, New York (arranged by Howard Putzel) : 1944, 1945
Mortimer Brandt Gallery, New York: Abstract and Surrealist Art in America (group show arranged by Sidney Janis), 1944
Betty Parsons Gallery, New York: 1946, 1947
Kootz Gallery, New York: 1947, 1949, 1950, 1951, 1952, 1953, 1954, 1955
Addison Gallery of American Art, Andover, Massachusetts (retrospective) : 1948
Art Institute of Chicago: Abstract and Surrealist American Art (group show), 1950
Galerie Maeght, Paris (arranged by Kootz Gallery) : 1949
Boston Arts Festival (outdoor group show) : 1951
Wildenstein Gallery, New York: 70 American Paintings 1900–1952 (group show), 1952
Museum of Modern Art, New York: Abstract Painting and Sculpture in America (group show), 1952
Boris Mirski Gallery, Boston: 1954
Sidney Janis Gallery, New York: Nine Americans (group show), 1954
Baltimore Museum of Art: 1954
Bennington College, Bennington, Vermont (retrospective) : 1955
Pennsylvania Academy of the Fine Arts, Philadelphia (group show) : 1956
Art Alliance, Philadelphia (retrospective) : 1956
Rutgers University, New Brunswick, New Jersey: 1956
Whitney Museum of American Art, New York (retrospective) : 1957

## WORKS IN PUBLIC COLLECTIONS

Addison Gallery of American Art, Andover, Massachusetts
Albright Art Gallery, Buffalo
Art Institute of Chicago
Baltimore Museum of Art
Blanden Memorial, Fort Dodge, Iowa
Metropolitan Museum of Art, New York
Museum of Modern Art, New York
University of Illinois Art Collection, Champaign-Urbana
University of Nebraska Art Galleries, Lincoln
Walker Art Center, Minneapolis
Washington University, St. Louis
Whitney Museum of American Art, New York

BURST INTO LIFE, 1952
Mrs. Pauling Donnelley, Chicago

# SELECTED BIBLIOGRAPHY

## BOOKS

Cheney, Sheldon. *Expressionism in Art*. New York: Liveright, 1934. Pp. 113, 156, 159, 160, 176, 186, 212.

Hess, Thomas. *Abstract Art*. New York: Lee Ault, 1951. Pp. 126–131.

Hofmann, Hans. *Search for the Real*. Andover, Massachusetts: Addison Gallery of American Art, 1948. Edited by Sarah T. Weeks and Bartlett H. Hayes, Jr. Introduction by Bartlett H. Hayes, Jr. Pp. 7–16.

Janis, Sidney, *Abstract and Surrealist Art in America*. New York: Reynal and Hitchcock, 1944. Pp. 48, 50, 51, 79.

Motherwell, Robert B. *Modern Artists in America*. New York: Wittenborn, 1952. Pp. 10–20, 106.

Ritchie, Andrew Carnduff. *Abstract Painting and Sculpture in America*. New York: Museum of Modern Art, 1951. P. 120.

Szittya, Emile. *L'Art Allemand en France*. 1927.

## ARTICLES

Bird, Paul. "Hofmann Profile," *Art Digest*, May 15, 1951, pp. 6–7.

de Kooning, Elaine. "Hans Hofmann Paints a Picture," *Art News*, February 1950, pp. 38–41, 58–59.

Ellsworth, Paul (assembled by). "Reply to Questionnaire and Comments on a Recent Exhibition," *Arts and Architecture*, November 1949, pp. 22–28+.

Estienne, Charles. "Hofmann ou La Lumière Américaine," *Derrière Le Miroir* (publication of the Galerie Maeght, Paris) January 1949 [no page numbers].

Fitzsimmons, James. "Exhibition at the Kootz," *Arts and Architecture*, July 1953, p. 10.

Greenberg, Clement. "Most Important Teacher of Our Time," *The Nation*, April 21, 1945, p. 469.

———. "The Present Prospects of American Painting and Sculpture," *Horizon*, October 1947, pp. 20–30.

———. "Feeling Is All," *Partisan Review*, January–February 1952, pp. 97–102.

———. "American Type Painting," *Partisan Review*, Spring 1955, pp. 179–196.

Kees, Weldon. "Weber and Hofmann," *Partisan Review*, May 1949, pp. 541–542.

Kepes, Gyorgy. "Review of *Search for the Real*," *Magazine of Art*, March 1952, p. 136.

Lawson, John Howard. "Hans Hofmann Exhibition at Art of This Century," *Arts and Architecture*, March 1944, pp. 23–26.

Matter, Mercedes. "Hans Hofmann," *Arts and Architecture*, May 1946, pp. 26–28+.

Neagoe, Peter. "Hans Hofmann," *Derrière Le Miroir*, January 1949.

Plaskett, Joe. "Some New Canadian Painters and Their Debt to Hans Hofmann," *Canadian Art*, Winter 1953, pp. 59–63+.

Putzel, Howard, "Art of This Century Exhibition," *Art News*, March 15, 1944, p. 20.

Sahl, Hans. "Kunst in New York," *Neu Züricher Zeitung*, November 28, 1952, p. 13.

Seckler, Dorothy. Interview: "Can Painting Be Taught?" *Art News*, March 1951, p. 40.

Sorzano, Margot. "Seventeen Modern American Painters," *Arts and Architecture*, January 1951, p. 26.

Willard, Charlotte. "Living in a Painting," *Look Magazine*, July 28, 1953, pp. 52–55.

Williams, Tennessee. "An Appreciation," *Derrière Le Miroir*, January 1949.

"Art in America," *Art Digest*, August 4, 1930, p. 27.

*Bennington College Alumnae Quarterly*, (Hofmann was asked to explain his own paintings), Autumn 1955, p. 25.

"Hofmann at Chouinard," *Art Digest*, February 15, 1931, p. 29.

"Muralist and the Modern Architect, The," *Arts and Architecture*, April 1951, pp. 18–19.

"Trapezoids and Empathy," *Time*, December 3, 1951, p. 72.


## EXHIBITION CATALOGUES

Art Institute of Chicago. *Abstract and Surrealist American Art*. Chicago, 1951. (Plate 118.)

Art of This Century. *First Exhibition-Hans Hofmann*. New York, 1944.

Art Students League. *Fifty Years on 57th Street*. New York, 1943.

Arts Club of Chicago. *Hans Hofmann*. Chicago, 1944.

Bennington College. Catalogue contains a critical essay by Clement Greenberg. Bennington, Vermont, 1955.

California Palace of the Legion of Honor. *Fourth Annual Exhibition of Contemporary American Painting*. San Francisco, 1951.

Galerie de France. *Regard sur la Peinture Américain*. Paris, 1953.

Mortimer Brandt Gallery. *Abstract and Surrealist Art in America*. New York, 1944.

Museum of Modern Art. *Abstract Painting and Sculpture in America*. New York, 1951. (*See under* Books.)

Rutgers University. Catalogue contains a critical essay by Allan Caprow. New Brunswick, New Jersey, 1956.

University of Illinois. *Contemporary American Painting*. Champaign-Urbana, 1951, 1952, 1953, 1955.

University of Minnesota. *40 American Painters*. Minneapolis, 1951.


## PUBLISHED WRITINGS BY THE ARTIST

Addison Gallery of American Art: *Search for the Real*. Introduction by Bartlett H. Hayes, Jr. Edited by Sarah T. Weeks and Bartlett H. Hayes, Jr. Andover, Massachusetts, 1949.

*Arts and Architecture:* "The Color Problem in Pure Painting—Its Creative Origin," February 1956, pp. 14–15, 33–34.

*Fortnightly:* "On the Aims of Art" (trans. by Ernest Holz and Glenn Wessels), February 26, 1932, pp. 7–11.

———: "Painting and Culture" (as communicated to Glenn Wessels), September 11, 1931, pp. 5–7.

New Ventures: "The Resurrection of the Plastic Arts," July 1953, pp. 20–22.

———: "The Mystery of Creative Relations," July 1953, pp. 22–23.

University of Illinois: Catalogue of "Contemporary American Painting" 1951, p. 187; 1952, p. 199; 1953, p. 189; 1955, p. 207.

*The League:* "Plastic Creation" (trans. from the German) Winter 1932–1933, reprinted Winter 1950, pp. 3–6. (Publication of the Art Students League, New York.)

# PAINTINGS AND DRAWINGS

HD1415 J63